5 Steps to
A Healthy and Positive Childhood

Learn about

5 Steps to
A Healthy and Positive
Childhood

Dr. ANJALI ARORA

Sterling Paperbacks

STERLING PAPERBACKS
An imprint of
Sterling Publishers (P) Ltd.
A-59, Okhla Industrial Area, Phase-II,
New Delhi-110020.
Tel: 26387070, 26386209; Fax: 91-11-26383788
E-mail: mail@sterlingpublishers.com
www.sterlingpublishers.com

5 Steps to
A Healthy and Positive Childhood
© 2010, *Dr. Anjali Arora*
arora_doc@hotmail.com
ISBN 978 81 207 4921 4

The author wishes to thank all academicians, scientists and writers who have been a source of inspiration.

The author and publisher specifically disclaim any liability, loss or risk, whatsoever, personal or otherwise, which is incurred as a consequence, directly or indirectly of
the use and application of any of the contents of this book.

All rights are reserved.
No part of this publication may be reproduced, stored in a retrieval system or transmitted, in any form or by any means, mechanical, photocopying, recording or otherwise, without prior written permission of the authors.

Printed and Published by Sterling Publishers Pvt. Ltd.,
New Delhi-110020.

Contents

1. Its All Starts from Motherhood 7
2. Breastfeeding and Immunisation 11
3. A Positive Childhood 24
4. Childhood Problems and Ailments 29
5. Healthy Childhood and Progressive Mind 57

   Myths and Fact File 69

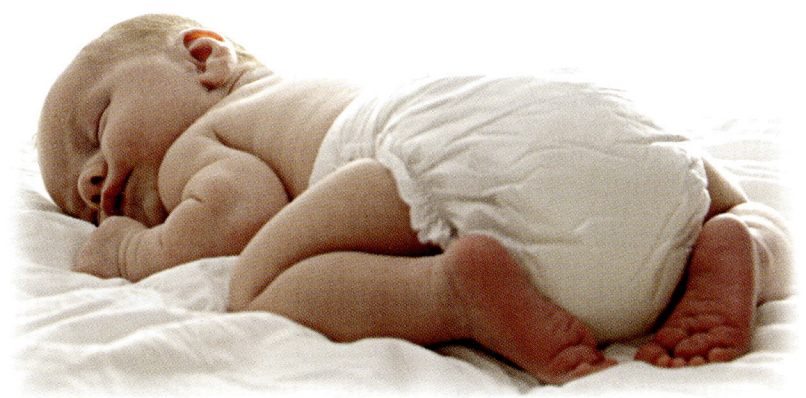

Are You Aware of Some of These Factors?

The birth of a healthy child is a lot dependent upon the mother's health during pregnancy.

1. **When a woman is pregnant she should not be deficient in**
a. Iron
b. Fats
c. Cholesterol

2. **On the birth of the baby, what score is important?**
a. Apgar
b. Lifestyle
c. Zenith

3. **Which is the first vaccine administered to the child after birth ?**
a. Hepatitis B
b. Measles
c. Mumps

4. **During pregnancy, which of the following shots is important for motherhood ?**
a. Tetanus
b. Thyroid
c. Chicken pox

The more times you tick (a) more are your chances of having a healthy baby.

Its All Starts from Motherhood

Childhood is where dreams begin. Often, with these dreams are associated factors of innocence, naivety and zest. How these factors translate over time eventually gives us the personality of the individual. Actually it all starts with the mother's pregnancy, how the little one does in the womb and then at birth. Later, it depends upon the formative years taking their toll or shielding the child from ailments and mental traumas. The age at which the child is considered responsible for his actions has also changed over centuries. This is due to the social attitude towards a child. A healthy childhood is protection, prevention, recovery and growth. It is a survival story – from the cocoon to the butterfly!

PRENATAL CARE

Care of a woman should begin even before she conceives. She should be physically and mentally mature for her first pregnancy.

Prenatal Advice

Prenatal advice consists of genetic counselling for the prospective parents and also guidance on natural nutrition, personal hygiene and protection of the unborn against intrauterine infections. Advice of no smoking and avoiding alcohol is a must. It should be remembered that a pregnancy in total duration consumes a number of calories over and above the normal metabolic requirements. The diet therefore must be more than adequate.

Health Care

Anemia

The major factors associated with anemia in the mother are iron and folic acid deficiencies. It is well known that anemia during pregnancy often results in a high incidence of premature births and other diseases.

Antenatal Visits

1. First antenatal visit to the doctor should be as soon as the pregnancy is detected.
2. Thereafter the pregnant women's doctor or gynaecologist guides her for the following nine months of pregnancy.

Apgar Score

The apgar test is usually given to your baby twice: once at 1 minute after birth, and again at 5 minutes after birth.

Apgar stands for: Activity, Pulse, Grimace, Appearance and Respiration

Five factors used to evaluate the baby's condition are:

- Activity and muscle tone
- Pulse (heart rate)
- Grimace response (medically known as "reflex irritability")
- Appearance (skin coloration)
- Respiration (breathing rate and effort)

Each factor is scored on a scale of 0 to 2, with 2 being the best score.

A baby who scores a 7 or above on the test at 1 minute after birth is generally considered in good health. After 5 minutes of birth, the Apgar score is recalculated and should be 7 or above otherwise your baby will be closely monitored by the pediatrician.

HIV and the Newborn

HIV infection is a source of great concern especially in a newborn with an HIV positive mother. About 30 per cent babies born to HIV positive mothers get infected. Transmission of infection mostly occurs at the end of the pregnancy. There is also a risk of transmission of HIV infection through breast milk.

Age related development phases of a child

- Infancy (upto 1 year of age)
    - Neonatal period (first 28 days of life)
    - Post-neonatal period (from 28th day to 1 year)
- Pre-school age (1- 4 years)
- School age – early childhood (4-9 years)
- Middle childhood (9-11 years)
- Puberty and adolescence (9-18 years)

2 Breastfeeding and Immunisation

Breastfeeding

Babies have a natural sucking reflex that enables them to suck and swallow milk. Breastfeeding can be initiated within an hour of the birth of the child. Barring a few exceptions, human breast milk is considered the best source of nourishment for human infants.

Breast Milk

The first milk is called 'colostrum'. It is the most suitable food for the baby during the early period. It also has a high concentration of protein nutrients and anti-infective factors. These factors help the baby against respiratory infections and diarroheal diseases.

The breast milk composition of water, fat and other nutrients varies depending upon the mother's food consumption and environment.

Foremilk, released at the beginning of a feed is watery, low in fat and high in carbohydrates. Hindmilk, released as the feed progresses, is creamier. The fat content of the milk is primarily determined by the emptiness of the breast. The less milk in the breast, the higher the fat content.

Benefits of breastfeeding

For the mother

- Breastfeeding the baby soon after giving birth increases the mother's oxytocin levels. Increased oxytocin levels helps the mother's uterus to contract more quickly thus reducing bleeding. This helps in prevention of postpartum haemorrhage.
- Breastfeeding also releases the hormones oxytocin and prolactin which help the mother relax.
- As fat accumulated during pregnancy is used to produce milk, breastfeeding can help mothers lose weight.
- Frequent breastfeeding can delay the return of ovulation.
- Breastfeeding mothers have less risk of breast, ovarian, endometrial cancer and osteoporosis.

- Breastfeeding benefits mother and child both physically and psychologically.
- Beneficial hormones are released into the mother's body. The bond between the baby and mother strengthens during breastfeeding.

For the infant

Breastfed babies have a lower risk of sudden infant death syndrome. Essential nutrients and antibodies pass to the baby from the mother. Breastfeeding is associated with a lower risk of a number of diseases in the infants:

- Atopic disease – The onset of atopic dermatitis, cow milk allergy and wheezing in early childhood is delayed or prevented till about 4 months of age.
- Autoimmune thyroid disease
- Bacterial meningitis - Breast feeding is protective for infants under 6 months of age.

Some other diseases which are seen less in breast fed babies are

- Coeliac disease, Diabetes, Diarrhoea, Eczema, Obesity. Also Less common in breastfed children are Otitis media (middle ear infection), respiratory infection and wheezing.

- Urinary tract infection (UTI): Breastfeeding gives the baby's body a strong defence against a UTI immediately after his/her birth. Defence against this infection decreases around 7 months of age. Breast milk also has several anti-infective factors, including the anti-amoebic factor.

Expressing Breast Milk

When direct breastfeeding is not possible, a mother can express (artificially remove and store) her milk. With the help of a manual massage or the use of a breast pump, a woman can express her milk. She can keep this in freezer in storage bags, or in a bottle ready for use. Breast milk can be kept at room temperature for up to ten hours, refrigerated for up to eight days or frozen for up to four to six months. Expressed breast milk is also useful for babies who are ill and are unable to be fed. Expressed milk can also be used when a mother is having trouble breastfeeding. This can be due to breast infection through grazing and bruising of the breast, by the newborn.

Time for breastfeeding

Breastfeeding at least once every two to three hours helps to maintain milk production. Feeding the baby on demand (sometimes is referred to as 'on cue'), means breastfeeding much more than the minimum recommended amount. Feeding when the baby shows early signs of hunger is the best way to maintain milk production.

Breastfeeding often makes the mother thirsty. Drinking enough water can help the mother maintain proper hydration.

Position of the mother during breastfeeding

While most women breastfeed their child in the cradling position, there are many other ways to hold the feeding baby.

- **Upright**: The sitting position with the back straight and leaning back comfortably.
- **Mobile**: The mother carries her baby in a sling or a baby carrier while breastfeeding.
- **Lying down**: Good for night feeds or for those who have had a caesarean section.
- **On her back:** Mother usually sits slightly upright. This position is particularly useful for tandem breastfeeding. It also helps when nursing more than one child.
- **On her side:** The mother and baby lie on their sides.
- **Cradle hold:** The baby is held with its head on the woman's tummy horizontally across the abdomen, 'tummy to tummy'. The woman should be in an upright and supported position.

- **Cross-cradle hold:** As shown earlier, the baby is held with its head in the woman's hand.

Mixed feeding

Predominant or mixed breastfeeding means feeding breast milk along with infant formula, baby food and even water, depending on the age of the child.

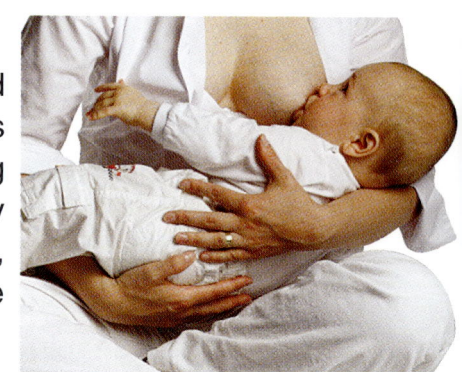

Tandem breastfeeding

Feeding two children at the same time is called *tandem* breastfeeding. The most common reason for tandem breastfeeding is the birth of twins.

Infant weight gain

A child's physical growth refers to the increase in height and weight, including other body changes. An average breastfed baby doubles his birth weight in 5 to 6 months. By one year, a breastfed baby should weigh about 2½ times more than the weight at birth. At one year, breastfed babies tend to be leaner than bottle fed babies.

Weaning

Weaning is the process of introducing the infant to ordinary food and reducing the supply of breast milk. The infant is fully weaned once it relies on ordinary food for all its nutrition and no longer receives any breast milk.

Diapering a Baby

Wiping

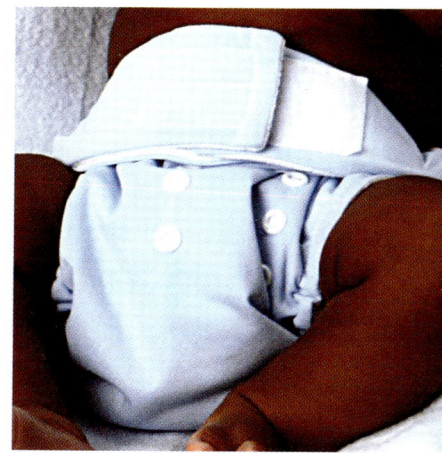

Babies can be wiped using the wet washcloth, cotton balls, or baby wipes. Gently wipe the baby clean from the front to the back (never wipe from back to front, especially a girl. You could spread the bacteria that can cause urinary tract infections forward from the rectum). For the baby boy, it's a good idea to keep a clean diaper over the penis during changing as exposure to the air often causes urination. Once you've finished wiping, pat your baby dry with a clean washcloth and if required apply a diaper ointment.

Caution

- While fastening the diaper, be careful not to stick the tape onto the baby's skin.
- If there are any marks around the baby's legs and waist, this would indicate that the diaper is too tight. Try getting a looser fit.

- If a rash develops at the diaper openings around the baby's leg and waist, change the brand of the diaper you are using.
- Garbage should be emptied at least once a day if disposables are being used. This would prevent any growth of bacteria around the baby.
- While diapering a boy, place the penis in a downward position before fastening the diaper.
- Always wash your hands after changing your baby's diaper. This helps to prevent the spread of germs.

Cloth Diapers

- When using diapers that require pinning, use oversized pins with plastic safety heads.
- Wet diapers can be tossed right into the diaper pail, but soiled diapers should be rinsed before washing. Diapers could also be sprayed with water and baking soda for better odour control (or put in dettol water).
- Diapers should be washed separately from other laundry. A mild detergent that is not allergic for the infant, should be used. Double rinse each wash, in hot water and dry the diapers in the sun.

Preventing Diaper Rash

- Change the baby's diapers frequently, especially after bowel movements.
- Let your baby go undiapered for sometime in the day.

- Use a diaper ointment to prevent and heal rashes.
- It's not uncommon for babies to have diaper rash. If the rash is persistent and lasts for more than 3 days, call up your doctor.

Your newborn baby and his/her bath

Once you have decided to give the baby a bath, get the bathing supplies together

- Soft towel
- Soft wash cloth
- Diaper
- Clothing
- A bowl full of warm water

Then, lay the baby on the towel. Talk to the baby while bathing. Do not frighten him. Moisten a soft towel with warm water. Wash the baby from head to toe. Begin with the child's face. Wash the eyes, ears, and nose first. Wash the genitals taking care to wash from front to back with girls and under the scrotum for boys. After washing lay the baby down, diaper and clothe him. Lotion is optional. Do not use powders. It can easily irritate the newborn's lungs. Remember never leave a baby alone during a bath.

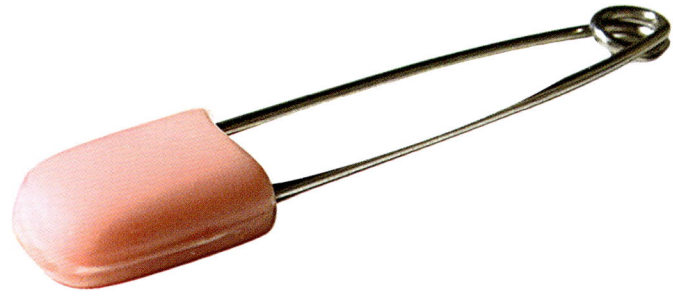

The baby's own space...

Nursery

The nursery has to be fancy or simple, according to your budget. Some basic requirements are important in a baby's room.

- Nursery should be next to or near the parents bedroom. It is important to hear the baby call or cry.
- The cot with an adjustable height mattress is useful.
- A changing table next to the cot would be convenient. Keep storage space under the table for nappies and towels.
- Shelves to be provided for the babies clothes. You can also put them in a basket.

- Basket – for soiled nappies, towels and sheets.
- Toys can be stored in a basket or brightly coloured box.

- Indirect lighting is best. Avoid bright lights.
- Windows for natural light / insect screen and prepainted grills.
- A comfortable chair where you can nurse the baby.

For Toddlers and Small Children

Be careful with electricity

- Protect all power points and cover them with safety socket covers.
- There should be no loose wiring around.
- Keep light fittings out of small children's reach.
- Ceiling fans are preferable to pedestal fans.

Furniture

- No sharp edged furniture
- Bookshelves should be secured to the walls

Window security

- Windows must have security locks
- The windows can be fitted with grills

Clothes

Clothes should be made of cotton or natural fibre. Synthetic fibers are highly inflammable. They are dangerous near open fires or flames from gas or oil heaters.

As the child grows up and goes to a proper school, the ambience of the nursery can change into a study cum play cum sleeping room.

Preventive Treatment for the Baby

Immunisation is a key for protection of the infant.

The Vaccination Regimen

Vaccinations are some of the most important tools available for preventing diseases. If enough people are immunised, the disease cannot be transmitted thus protecting everyone. Parents should consult their doctors about which vaccines their children should have and when. Keep a track of your child's immunisations yourself. **Do not misplace the vaccination card.**

The immunisation schedule may vary depending upon where you live, your child's health and the type available. The schedule is normally given to you by your doctor. The following vaccination are administered within first twelve months of the baby's birth:-

- **Hep B:** Hepatitis B vaccine is given at birth.

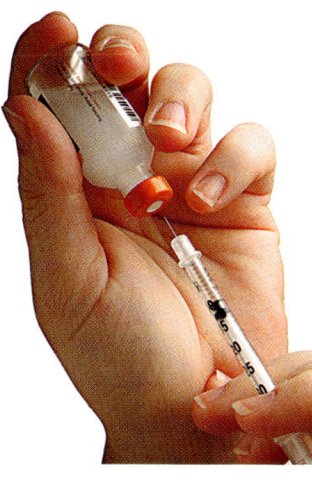

At 2 months

- **DTaP:** Diphtheria, tetanus, and acellular pertussis vaccine
- **Hib:** Haemophilus influenzae type b vaccine
- **IPV:** Inactivated poliovirus vaccine
- **PCV:** Pneumococcal conjugate vaccine
- **RV:** Rotavirus vaccine, recommended for infants at 2, 4, and 6 months of age
- **Influenza.** Influenza vaccine is recommended every year for high-risk children older than 6 months.
- **MMR:** Measles, mumps, and rubella (German measles) vaccine (12-15 months)
- **Var:** Varicella (chickenpox) vaccine may be given at any visit after first year. A second dose should be given between 4 and 6 years of age.
- **Hep A:** Hepatitis A vaccine is recommended for kids 12–23 months old, given as two shots with a gap of 6 months.

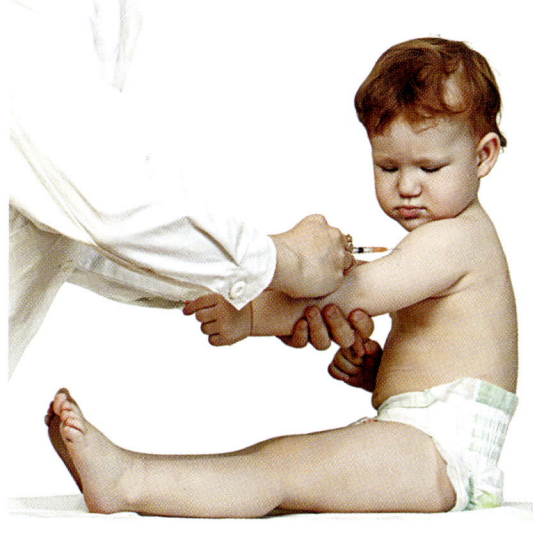

3   *A Positive Childhood*

Toilet training (or potty training)

It is the process of weaning a young child off diapers. Toilet training is usually started and completed between the age of eighteen months and four years. The child is ready when he or she can signal that the diaper is wet or soiled. This usually occurs when a child  is 18 to 24 months of age. However, a child may still be in diapers between two and a half to 3 years of age.

A normal child has bowel movement once a day, usually within an hour after eating. Most children urinate within 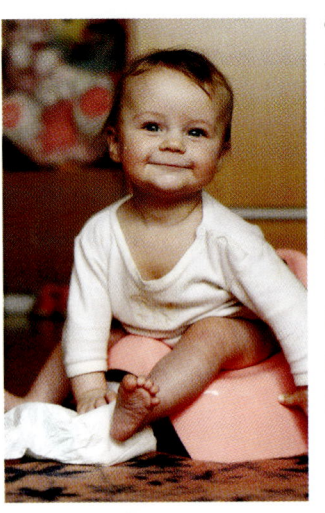 an hour after having a large drink. Signals show that your child needs to urinate or have a bowel movement. It helps to place the child on the potty at regular intervals. This may be as often as every one and a half to two hours.

Stay with the child when he or she is on the potty chair. If the child does not urinate or have a bowel movement in the potty do not get upset. Be patient

with the child. If the child is not toilet trained within 3 months of toilet training, consult your family doctor.

To survive in society and environment a child has to go through certain skills which come under normal parameters.

Speech and language

Speech and language are means through which humans communicate or share thoughts, ideas, and emotions.

The period during which the brain develops and matures is in the first three years of life. Consistent exposure to speech and language of others helps these skills develop early in a child. A natural 'timeframe' is marked for development of these skills. Milestones are identifiable skills that serve as a guide for normal development. These are:-

- **Gross motor:** Using large groups of muscles which are used to sit, stand, walk, run, keeping balance, and changing positions.
- **Fine motor:** Using hands to be able to eat, draw, etc.
- **Language:** Speaking, using gestures, communicating, and understanding.
- **Cognitive:** Thinking skills, including learning, understanding and remembering.
- **Social:** Interacting with others, cooperating, and responding.

Language Development

At 6 months of infancy
- Vocalisation with intonation
- Respond to name and human voices by turning his head and eyes

At 12 months of infancy
- Uses one or more words with meaning
- Understands simple instructions

At 18 months of infancy
- Is able to follow simple commands
- Much jargon, has vocabulary of approximately 5-20 words

At 24 months (2 years)
- Volume and pitch of voice not yet well-controlled

At 36 months (3 years)
- Understands most simple questions dealing with his environment and activities.

At 48 months (4 years)
- Knows names of familiar animals and objects in books

At 60 months (5 years)
- Speech intelligible, in spite of articulation problem
- Is able to define common objects in terms of use (e.g. shoe, chair)
- Uses longer sentences

Pre-School Age

Walking

When it comes to milestones, baby's first steps get imbedded in the parent's memory forever! They are there to cherish. The child's first steps are, after all, his first major move towards independence. During his first year, the baby is busy developing coordination and muscle strength throughout his body. The child learns to sit, roll over, and crawl before moving on to pulling up and standing at about 8 months. Most babies take their first steps sometime between 9 and 12 months. By the time they are 14 or 15 months old they start walking. Some children don't walk until they're 16 or 17 months old. Don't panic. Consult your doctor for guidance.

Your Role as a Parent

As the baby learns to pull himself up to a standing position, he may need some help. He may try and figure out how to get back down again. He may cry for you, don't just pick him up and plop him down. Show him how to bend his knees so that he can sit down without toppling over. Let him try it himself. Make sure your baby has a safe environment to hone his new skills.

Remember babies have different timetables. Premature babies may reach milestones later than their peers.

4   Childhood Problems and Ailments

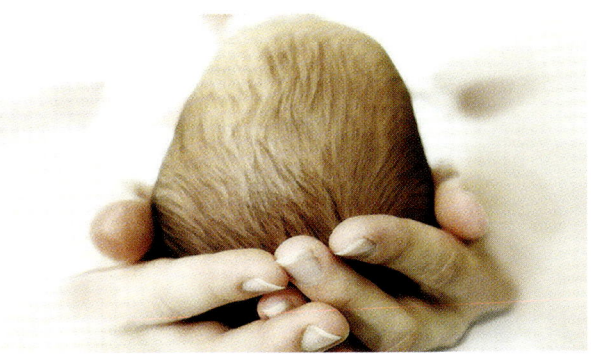

From the moment a baby arrives, parents eagerly watch his progress and observe and enjoy each milestone reached. At the same time, whenever required it becomes important to tend to any ailment of the child. It is also vital to differentiate between ailments being treatable at home or need the help of the local doctor or pediatrician.

Feeding the Baby

If you are breastfeeding, observe the length of time your baby takes to be breastfed. Also check whether sucking for milk is strong. Has he consumed the usual amount of milk?

Vomiting

Small amount of milk that comes out after a feed is considered normal.

Large amount of vomit after a couple of feeds should be taken seriously. If the baby vomits a green fluid, consult your pediatrician or doctor.

Urine and Stool

If there is less intake of milk and the baby vomits, less wet nappies will be seen. If less urine is passed by a baby over a period of time, it should be observed, and the doctor informed.

Blood in a baby's stool is a cause of concern. Consult a paediatrician.

Baby Blues

Rash

Few small spots of rash sometimes develop in babies. A large area of rash or number of spots present, especially if sore, should be looked into.

Shallow Breathing

A less responsive or drowsy baby has to be observed. Is he more irritable? Is his cry weak? Is this behavioural change going on for sometime? If so, these signs should be noted and reported to your doctor.

Babies often breathe shallowly. A baby sucking in the chest or upper part of tummy while breathing or wheezing should be reported to your doctor.

Shock

Shock in a baby might occur due to a bad fright. It can also be as a result of impaired circulation or improper breathing after an accident. Usually on squeezing your baby's big toe for a couple of seconds, a pale patch will develop. Upon releasing the toe, the colour will come back. If the colour is not revived within 3-4 seconds then it means that the circulation is slow. Also if a bluish colour develops on the baby's fingers or toes consult your doctor.

Initial Remedy

- Make the child lie down such that the head is lower than the feet.
- Take care of the child's breathing. It should not be obstructed by tight clothes or vomiting.
- If the child is not better within fifteen minutes, see your doctor.

Bulge

If your baby on crying develops a bulge in the groin or scrotum which disappears on sleep, consult your doctor. He or she probably has hernia.

Sore buttocks

Sore buttocks are normally due to nappy rash. Diarrhoea following unsuitable food can cause the buttocks to be red and sore. Worms can also lead to sore buttocks in children.

Choking

Children are prone to choke on small things. It is not advisable to leave small objects around a child.

Coughing out normally brings up the object. If the child turns blue rush him to the doctor.

Before taking the child to a doctor:-

- Check if you can see the object. Try dislodging it with your finger.
- If not, put him across your knees, lower his head lower than his legs. Pat him firmly between the shoulder blades.
- If the object still cannot be removed call an ambulance or rush the child to the nearest medical centre.

Necessary aids required in a home with a child

First-aid Box

- Cotton wool
- Sterile gauze packet
- Sticking plasters
- Roll of sticking plaster (to cover larger cuts)
- Pair of small scissors and tweezers
- Safety pins
- Crepe bandage for sprain
- A couple of gauze bandages for dressing
- Triangular bandage for sling

Your doctor's phone number and address should be stuck on top of your first-aid box.

Medicine Pack

- Paracetamol suspension
- Nappy rash cream
- Calamine lotion for rashes and bites
- Multivitamin drops or capsules
- Antiseptic lotion to clean grazes and cuts
- Cream for burns for infants / tablets for children
- Plastic spoon (5 ml)
- Vapour chest rub

A Word of Caution

- Your first-aid box and medicine pack should be out of reach of children.
- See that the child cannot reach it by climbing on your bed or stool.
- Dispose of all old medicines.
- Eye drops and nose drops should be thrown once the child is cured.

Temperature

A newborn's and baby's normal temperature is 37.5 °C (98.4 °F). There is a difference in temperature at different sites of the body. Under the arm it is lower and if the temperature is taken in the rectum it is higher.

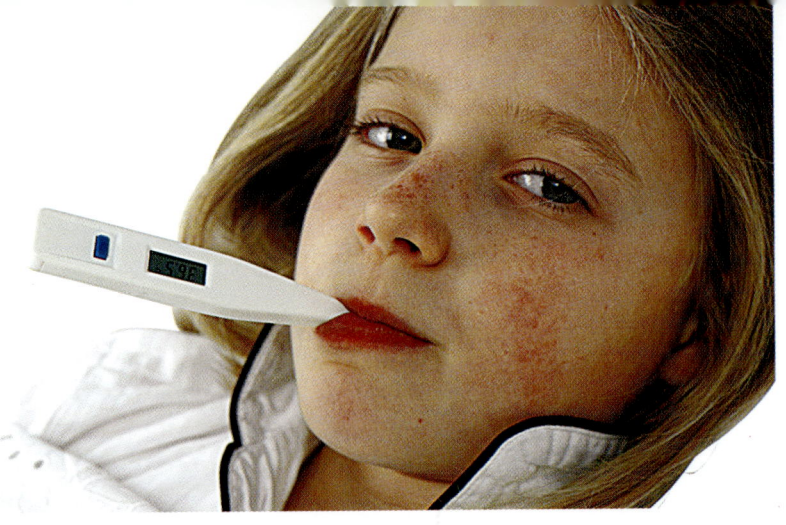

Temperature above 38.3°C (101°F) should be reported to the doctor to correlate it with other signs.

Fever

If a child looks flushed and feels unwell, take his/her temperature.

- Do not wrap him up with too many clothes.
- Make the room comfortable at 25°C (77°F) approximately.
- Ventilate the room properly.
- Put him into bed and give him plenty of drinks. Do not let him get dehydrated.
- Give the dosage of paracetamol recommended.
- If the temperature still rises, give him a cold sponge.

Cold sponge

- Spread a plastic or rubber sheet on the bed. Avoid the sheets from getting wet.
- Prepare a bowl of cold water and sponge the child's forehead, neck, palms and feet.

- If the temperature does not come down, then undress the child and also sponge him under his arms or groin.

Cold sponging can have a quick effect in lowering the temperature. You can leave a cool small towel on his forehead and neck, which is refreshed frequently. Check the child's temperature every 10 to 15 minutes. To stop sponging, the temperature should come down to 37.8°C (100°F). High temperature can lead to convulsions.

Convulsions

Babies or small children often convulse due to high temperature. The baby becomes rigid and then his muscles clench and unclench with jerks and twitches.

Remember

- Do not leave the baby alone
- Phone for help
- Ensure that he does not inhale any vomit
- Try to keep him or his head on one side

Convulsions lasts only a few minutes. Children normally fall asleep after that.

Nosebleeds

- Nosebleeds can become terrifying for a child. First, wash the blood away.
- Tilt the child's head at the back and pinch the nostrils for 2 minutes. The blood will have a chance to clot.

- Do not let the child pick or blow his nose for at least an hour after the bleeding has stopped.

Abdominal pain in children

Abdominal pain is a symptom which is seen in a majority of cases. It is normally due to a harmless cause but can become significant in a number of cases. In only a few cases does abdominal pain become an emergency.

Common Causes of Abdominal Pain

- ### Indigestion

It is commonly known as 'tummy upset'. This is caused by wrong eating habits like overeating, drinking too many fizzy drinks or eating junk food.

Remedy: Drinking warm water, keeping a hot water bottle over the stomach or taking antacids often helps to relieve the pain.

- ### Constipation

The stools can be hard, dry and scanty. This may cause stomachache, nausea and vomiting.

Remedy: A high fibre diet (more of salads, fruits, etc), and gentle laxatives help to relieve this condition.

- Gastroenteritis

It may be caused due to a viral or bacterial infection. It may present itself with diarrhoea which is associated with severe abdominal cramps, vomiting and fever.

Remedy: Stool examination and medication are needed.

- Worm infestation

It is mostly caused by round worms. It can cause recurrent stomachache in children.

Remedy: A course of anti-worm medications usually cures the infection. Stool examination should be done three times.

Home remedy for abdominal pain

- Let the child lie down and rest. Keep a warm water bottle or heating pad on the stomach for 20 minutes till the pain subsides.
- Give only sips of clear fluids, but no solids. Keep a vomiting pan handy.
- Encourage the child to sit on the toilet and try to pass stool. This often relieves the pain.
- No medications should be given without the doctor's advice. Pain killers often mask a more serious illness like appendicitis.

Harmless pain usually gets better or disappears in about 2 hours. If the pain lasts for more than three hours, a doctor should be consulted.

- **Food allergies**

Abdominal pain can be due to allergy to certain food constituents, e.g. lactose in milk. Certain food preservatives (like colour) used in cold drinks or pickles can be a cause of stomachache in children.

Drugs

Epileptic or antimalarial drugs and some antibiotics may cause abdominal pain in children.

- **Chronic recurrent abdominal pain**

This type of pain is seen in late childhood (8-15 years). A physical cause should be excluded after thorough examination and investigations. If abdominal pain persists, and there is a history of three or more episodes of severe abdominal pain over a period of 3-4 months, the pain may be psychological in origin, caused by worry or anxiety.

Some Common Infectious Diseases

Measles

It is an infectious disease. Its virus is transmitted through air or water droplets. The incubation period is of 10 to 12 days after an exposure to the virus.

Symptoms

- Cold with running nose
- Sore eyes and fever

- Cough can be present
- White spots can be present inside the cheeks near the back molars.
- Heavy red rash behind the ears which spreads on the trunk and sometimes to the arms and legs.

Normally, the rash disappears within 3 to 4 days and so does the fever. If fever and rash do not subside or disappear and the child develops other symptoms, consult your doctor for complications.

Advice: During an attack of measles, cold drinks, light meals and plenty of rest is advised for the child. Fever and joint pains can be controlled by paracetamol.

Mumps

It is caused by a viral infection, which affects the salivary glands. It comes through the saliva of an already infected individual. Incubation of this disease is two to three weeks. Children over 5 years of age are normally affected by it.

Symptoms

- Fever
- Muscular pain in neck
- Headache
- Glands under the jaw can become swollen (lasts for 7-14 days)

If the child remains unwell, appears drowsy or remains off colour and in pain, consult your pediatrician.

Advice

Soft and cooked food. After meals give the child a mouthwash as gums can get infected. Paracetamol can be given to reduce the temperature. Keep the child isolated as others can get infected.

Rubella or German Measles

It is a very infectious disease. It is transmitted from one person to another by droplets or sputum through coughing. It can be transmitted indirectly through infected crockery, cutlery or certain items used by the affected person.

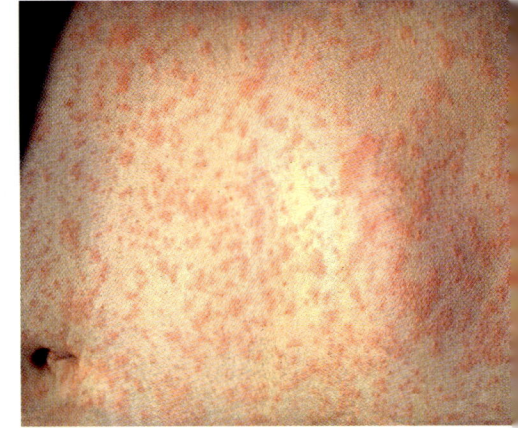

Symptoms

Incubation period is 14 to 21 days

- First sign of German measles is development of mild cattarh.
- Lymph nodes present behind the ears and at the back of the neck get swollen and tender.
- A few days later, rash is seen behind the ears and forehead which spreads to the body.
- The child may develop slight fever with rash lasting for 2-3 days.

Chicken Pox

Chicken Pox presents itself with headache and fever with swollen lymph nodes. A blotchy rash can appear 2-3 days later over the trunk. The rash is pimple like in nature. A day or so later, the rash dries off and falls in about 10 days time. If there is some infection (e.g. with pus) consult your pediatrician. In chicken pox the incubation period is of 17-21 days.

Advice

Use calamine lotion on the rash. This will help soothe the itchy area. Anti-histamine syrup/ tablet or a mild sedative can be advised for the child by your doctor.

Itchy skin and rash in a child can be due to some of these other conditions

- Heat rash, often called prickly heat
- Eczema
- Ringworm infection
- Allergy
- Herpes simplex

Other Childhood Problems

Poisoning

A child who has consumed poisonous substances or poison needs immediate attention.

- Clear his mouth of any tablets

- Check the bottle from which the poison has been consumed. It will help the doctor in the casualty to assess as to how much was consumed by the child.
- Some poisons should not be vomited. If they are acidic, they can cause further burning.
- The child must be rushed to the hospital as soon as possible. Poisoning is a medical emergency.

Splinters

Small splinters of wood in the skin can be taken out with the help of tweezers. If a stuck splinter is not painful, leave it. It will come out in due course. If a splinter of metal or glass is stuck consult your doctor. Do not attempt to remove it yourself.

Electrical shocks and burns

In case of an electrical shock first of all turn off the source of electricity before touching the child. There would be scalds on the skin surface and the child shocked and dazed. So take him to the doctor or hospital immediately.

Eye infections

- Conjunctivitis or sticky eye
- Blinking – When a child is mentally disturbed he can get into the habit of blinking. Blinking can also be due to an allergy or conjunctivitis.
- Stye – a small painful boil on the eyelid

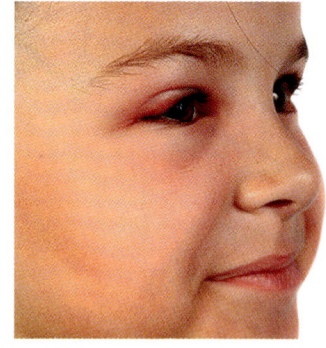

Conjunctivitis

Conjunctivitis is an inflammation of the conjunctivae. The conjunctivae are the mucous membranes covering the white of the eyes and the inner side of the eyelids. It usually affects both the eyes at the same time. If it starts with one eye it spreads to the other. Conjunctivitis can occur due to bacteria, virus, allergy or other causes.

Remedy: Conjunctivitis can usually be diagnosed and treated by the opthalmologist (eye doctor). Good hygiene of hands and face is important. There should be no sharing of face towels, especially if someone has been affected by conjunctivitis.

Blinking

Some causes of excessive blinking in a child can be:-

- Dry eyes
- Nervousness
- Infection
- Foreign body in the eye

An eye injury, accident or foreign body in the eyes should be examined by the eye specialist. It is an emergency.

Precautions:

- Do not let the child rub the eye. It can cause more injury.
- Wash the eye gently with tap water.
- Help the child keep his eyes closed till he sees the doctor.

Eye defects

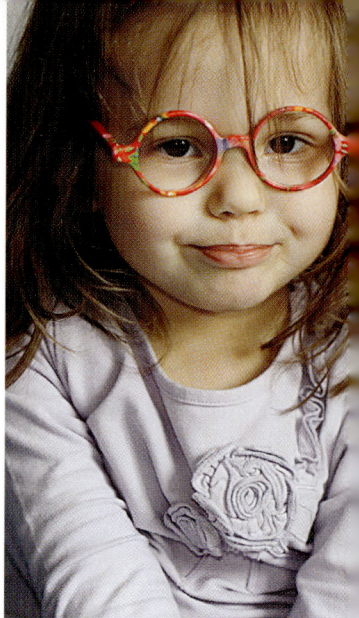

- Short sightedness is the inability to focus on far away objects. Near objects can be seen and focussed upon.
- Far sightedness is the inability to focus on near objects.
- Squint (Strabismus) is an abnormal condition, which makes the eyes look in different direction from each other.
- Nystagmus involves involuntary rapid movement of the eyeball.

Ear infections

The most common infections of the ear occur in the first year of a baby's life.

The opening of the ear leads to the eardrum, which is protected by secretion of wax. The other side of the eardrum is the middle ear. This is connected through

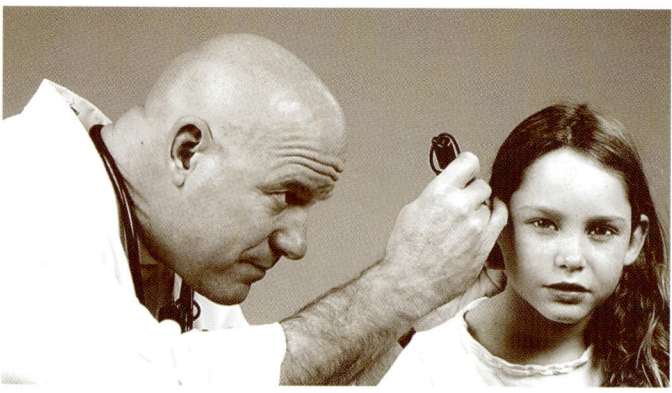

the eustachian tube to the back of the throat. The inner ear contains sensitive parts. It is the inner ear which is responsible for the hearing and balance.

Common Problems in children

- Discharge
- Earache
- Excess wax production
- Itching of the ear (can be due to allergy)

Problems can occur in all parts of the ear. Children while playing often insert a small object in their ear, nose or even mouth. This can be dangerous. Avoid leaving small objects around a child. Excess wax or boil can be painful for a child. These ailments should be treated with the help of your doctor. The most common cause of earache is due to middle ear infection. This occurs when your child is suffering from sore throats and cold. Earache also occurs with infectious diseases. In spite of treatment, if the pain persists, administer some paracetamol tablets or syrup to the child and then consult your doctor or ENT specialist.

Detection of a hearing problem or deafness

- The baby is startled by your appearance by his side.
- He does not turn towards any sound by 3 months of age

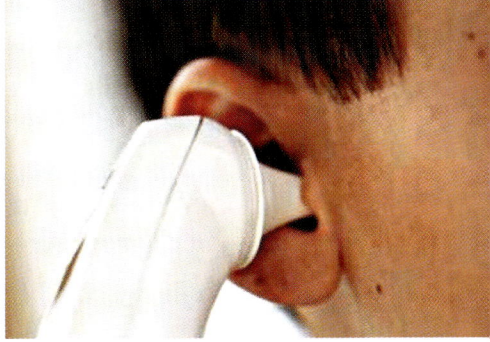

- The baby does not even utter a few words by 12 months of age.

Remember even the slightest degree of deafness in a child can interfere with his speech. Consult your pediatrician for guidance.

Allergies

Allergy or allergy like symptoms can be exacerbated in children. Factors leading to this can be:-

- **An infection**

    After a bad cold, infection of the stomach, or infantile eczema.

- **Weather**

    During spring, in a windy weather and sometimes due to the pollen in the air. During damp weather the presence of spores can cause allergy.

Emotional disturbance

Fear or distress can bring about an asthmatic attack in children.

Eczema

It is a disorder of infancy. In typical form, it is seen to set in the creases of the arms and back of legs. There is itchiness and the skin turns red.

Asthma

It can begin during infancy. A baby after lung infection due to flu, pneumonia or constant cold can show early signs of asthma. Asthma has to be diagnosed by your doctor. A few wheezes and sneezes do not indicate asthma.

Emotional stress itself (anxiety, frustration, anger) can trigger asthma, but the asthmatic condition precedes the emotional stress. Many children with asthma suffer from severe anxiety during an episode as a result of suffocation produced by the disease. The anxiety and panic can then produce rapid breathing or hyperventilation, which further triggers asthma. During an episode, anxiety and panic should be controlled as much as possible. The parent should help the child to relax, breathe easily and give medications as prescribed by the doctor.

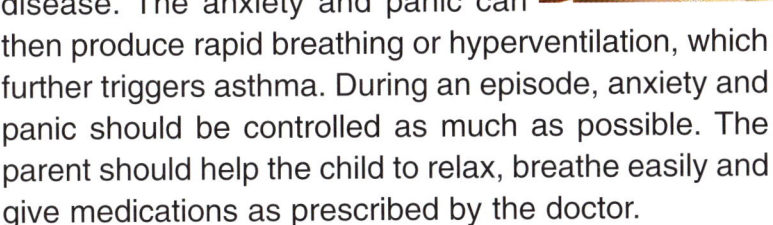

Remember
Asthma is an inflammatory condition of the airways caused by allergens, irritants and respiratory infections. It is triggered by many different stimuli (trigger factors).

Investigations
A variety of tests now exist to diagnose allergic conditions. Treatments for allergies include allergen avoidance, use of antihistamines, steroids or other oral medication.

Dental Health of Children
The first year of an infant's life is a time of tremendous change. Eruption of teeth causes the child to be cranky and irritable.

Natal Teeth

Natal teeth may be present when the infant is born. About one in every 2,000 newborn infants can have natal teeth. These teeth are usually the infant's primary teeth (or baby teeth) that have come in early.

Management of natal teeth

Teeth that are loose may need to be removed. This is to avoid the risk of the infant inhaling the tooth into his/her airways.

Epstein's Pearls

Epstein's pearls are a type of benign cyst (fluid-filled sac) that occur on the roof of the infant's mouth. Epstein's pearls are small, white bumps which are commonly seen in infants. They are harmless and improve over a period of weeks.

Eruption of Primary or Deciduous Teeth

	Upper	Lower
Central incisors	6-8 months	5-7 months
Lateral incisors	8-11 months	7-10 months
Canines	16-20 months	16-20 months
First molars	10-16 months	10-16 months
Second molars	20-30 months	20-30 months

(Adapted from chart prepared by PK Losch, Harvard School of Dental Medicine, from Nelson's Textbook of Pediatrics.)

In case a permanent tooth becomes visible before the primary tooth has fallen, the primary tooth should be extracted.

Coeliac Sprue

Coeliac sprue is an autoimmune disease of the intestines. Gluten, a protein found in various cereal grains gives rise to this condition. A child with coeliac disease should follow a gluten-free diet.

The principle sources of gluten in the diet include wheat, rye, and barley. Oats may be tolerated in small amounts.

To follow a gluten-free diet

First, read all the labels on prepared foods. Do not give the child any food containing the following:

- Hydrolysed vegetable protein
- Flour or cereal products

- Vegetable protein
- Malt and malt flavourings
- Starches (unless specified as corn starch, which does not contain gluten)
- Various flavourings, which can be derived from cereals containing gluten
- Vegetable gum
- Emulsifiers, stabilisers derived from cereals containing gluten

When a child is with you in a restaurant make him avoid:

- Breads
- Creamed foods
- Meatloaf and gravies
- Gluten which is also used in food in some unexpected ways for example as a stabilising agent or thickener.

Injuries

After finding their feet, children between 4-12 years of age are extremely active. They have boundless energy and want to move around non-stop. This often leads to injury.

Light bleeding or graze

Bleeding from a graze or light bleeding stops on its own after clot formation. In case it persists, press it firmly with a pad of cotton or clean gauze. Clean the area with an antiseptic and dress it with a sterile gauze, a sticking plaster or bandage it.

Caution

See that your child has had his tetanus immunisation. Check the child's immunisation period. In case it has expired, get another shot within 24 hours.

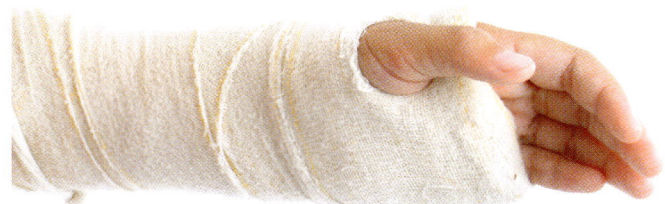

Fractures

Fractures can be common in young children. One of the commonest is the greenstick fracture. The limb may be swollen in case of a fracture.

- Make the child comfortable.
- Consult your doctor and take the child for an X-ray.
- Avoid moving the area of injury frequently.

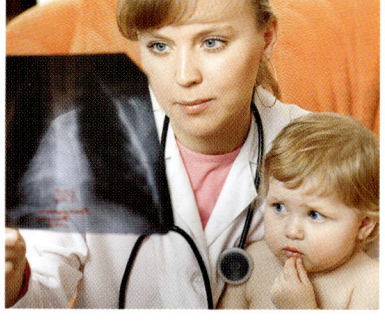

- If there is an open wound cover the area with a clean piece of gauze. Do not attempt to clean it in case it gets infected.

Injury can also occur on any part of the body, e.g. spine, hip bone, head.

Caution

Do not feed the child, in case he needs some form of surgery.

Head injury

In case of head injury, an ice pack should be used to ease the swelling

Observe the Child

- His face colour and breathing
- Vomiting
- Eye irregularity
- Hearing
- Mumbling speech
- Bleeding

Get the child examined by the doctor.

Heavy Bleeding

After an injury, blood dripping from the wound should be controlled as quickly as possible. Pressure applied to seal the cut edges of the wound help form a clot on the cut. If blood still spurts from the wound, raise the limb over the heart level and press on the wound. If spurting continues, find an area to press against the cut. Get immediate help and try and get the child to a medical center or hospital.

Caution

- If an object is sticking from the wound, do not try to remove it.
- Do not give the child any food or drink in case he is required to go to the operation theatre.

Burns in Children

Burns can be through accidents or their experimentation. They must be treated immediately. Burns are one of the most common causes of injury to children.

First-aid for burns

- Place the burned area under cool, running water. You could also dip a cloth in chilled water, and place it on the burn. Do not apply ice to the burn, it only increases the pain of the wound and does not help much.

- Remove any clothing from the burnt area immediately. Cut the clothing if you have to. If the clothing is stuck to the skin, which may be the case in second or third degree burns, do not remove it. If the burn is caused by a chemical, make sure you don't spread the chemical around when removing the clothing.
- Take care in not bursting any blisters which may have formed as a result of the burn.
- After cooling the burn for about fifteen minutes, you can apply an ointment specific to burns. Cover the burnt area with a piece of clean gauze.
- If your child's eyes get burnt, flush the eyes continuously with water, and call a doctor immediately.

The most important thing to remember is to cool the burn and to reduce damage to the skin and the underlying tissues. Get to your doctor or hospital as soon as possible.

Juvenile Diabetes

Juvenile diabetes is an autoimmune disorder. It can also be due to an environmental trigger or virus, which destroy the beta cells. Once the beta cells are destroyed the body is unable to produce insulin. A child with diabetic siblings is more prone to develop juvenile diabetes. The amount of insulin required to breakdown the sugar in the body is produced by the pancreas. A juvenile diabetic lacks the production of insulin. This insulin lack results in rise of blood sugar levels which pass into the urine unused.

Children get terrified with daily insulin injections. Parents of a child with Type 1 diabetes should not over react and in fact, be supportive of the child. The child should be encouraged to continue with normal social activities and stress. The child should not be made to feel that he or she is bad when they eat food which sometimes is not recommended or can cause high blood sugar levels. It is important to describe the result as high/low/normal and not as very good or bad. Explain things regularly and encourage and help the child in keeping the blood sugar within normal levels.

Symptoms of Juvenile Diabetics

- Increased thirst
- Increased hunger
- Increased urination
- Weight loss
- Fatigue
- Flu like symptoms
- Fruity breath odour
- Bedwetting

Treatment

Insulin - The only treatment for juvenile diabetes is insulin injections or an insulin pump.

Self-monitoring of blood glucose - As advised by the treating Pediatrician.

Exercise - Diet and exercise have a very significant role to play towards the treatment of diabetes.

Diabetic's diet

- Children with juvenile diabetes and their families should learn about different foods especially carbohydrates such as bread, pasta, and rice which can affect blood glucose levels.
- A child with type 1 diabetes should indulge in any physical activity regularly. This is essential in lowering blood glucose levels, controlling weight, and reducing stress.

5   *Healthy Childhood and Progressive Mind*

Developmental Milestones

In children 9-11 years of age healthy friendships are very important for the child's development. At this stage, the child tries to become independent. Physical changes of puberty start showing at this age, especially in girls. The girl or boy child may become more aware of his or her body as puberty approaches.

Safety of your child in the modern world

- Many children get home from school before their parents. It is important to have clear rules and plans for the child when he or she is alone at home.

- Know where the child is whenever he is out. Be clear, where you can find him, and what time you expect him home.
- Protect the child in the car. All children younger than 12 years of age should ride in the back seat with a seat belt properly fastened.

Positive Parenting

You can help the child become independent. It is important to build his or her sense of responsibility and self-confidence.

- Be involved with the child's academics and activities. Go to school events; meet the child's teachers.

- Spend time with the child. Talk with him or her about their friends, their accomplishments, and what challenges they will face.
- Help the child develop his own sense of right and wrong. Talk with him about peer pressure, harmful effects of smoking, drugs, etc.
- Help the child develop a sense of responsibility. Involve your child in household tasks.
- Encourage the child to respect others and help people in need.

Factors to keep in mind in the modern era .....

Eyestrain

1. Does the child read under proper light ?
2. Does he or she keep a right distance of 1 ft.approx between the eye and the book ?
3. Can he read the blackboard comfortably ?
4. Does he have an eye checkup yearly ?

Outdoor Activity

It is important for every child whatever his schedule may be. It creates a bonding with nature, makes a child physically fit and more balanced to deal with the daily pressures.

Strangers and Children

Parents should teach the child to be wary of strangers.

- To keep distance with a stranger, including street vendors.

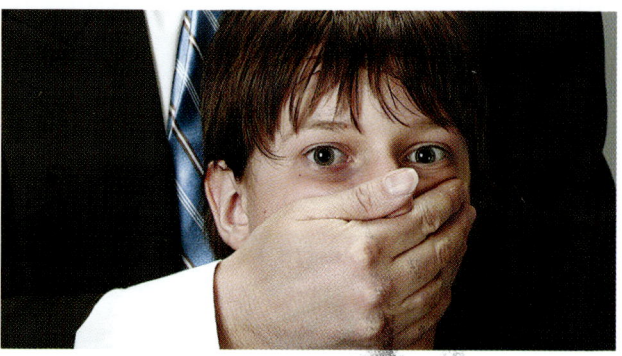

- Not allowing strangers to touch him or her.
- Should not go anywhere with a stranger (unless permission is granted by parents).

Child Abuse

Child abuse is the sexual maltreatment of children. It can be physical or psychological in nature. Psychological child abuse can occur in the child's home, in organisations like churches, schools and boarding schools. Physical abuse can be through striking, shaking, pinching, pulling hair or

ear. Sexual abuse can include violations of privacy, exposing children to adult sexuality and psychological exploitation.

Effects

Children with a history of neglect or physical abuse often develop psychiatric problems. This can present itself as anxiety, depressive or dissociative symptoms. Domestic violence is another area associated with depressive symptoms.

Sexual education is important

The teenager needs a different kind of guidance

- Help the child set his own goals. Encourage him to think about his skills, and how he would like to go about it.
- Let him learn about his abilities and limitations.
- Make clear rules and stick to them.
- Encourage the child to read every day.
- Be affectionate and honest with your child and do things together as a family.

A teenager definitely has different ideas. Adolescence – its moods, peer groups – pajama parties. Parents wonder as to where one should draw the line. On the otherhand, the teenager feels stifled among primitive thinking elders.

Children and the mobile phone

For a teenager a mobile phone or internet increases the opportunity to bond with friends. It has become important for a teenager's individuality and confidence. This culture of chatting on the phone for hours, however is not acceptable to most parents.

Concerns while using a mobile phone are

- ### Health risk (radiation)

Mobile usage should not be addictive. As the head and the nervous system is under development in the teenage years, children and young people might be more vulnerable to nerve damage than adults.

- ### Driving safety regulations

It is seen that a driver's reaction time is 30 per cent slower when talking on a mobile than under normal driving conditions. 'Hand free' mobile phones also affect drivers.

Sex Education

At puberty children need to be informed about their reproductive system. Parents should take it upon themselves to inform their children what sex and sexuality is all about.

Puberty

The changes which occur in the body, suddenly bring about a different individual. Puberty is a stage in a person's life when they develop from a child into an adult.

Puberty and Male Behaviour (10-18 years)

- Mood swings and more aggression
- Sleeps a lot
- Thinks and fantasies about sex
- Masturbates

Physical changes during puberty in the males

- Body growth
- Genitalia growth and pubic hair growth
- Possible breast development
- Voice change
- Growth of body hair
- Acne

Puberty and Female Behaviour (9-17 years)

- Mood swings
- Sleeps a lot
- Masturbates

Physical changes during puberty in females are:

Premenstrual syndrome (PMS) around the time of their periods can cause headaches, back pain, irritability or moodiness, feeling of sadness or disturbances, bloating, and breast tenderness.

Childhood Obesity

An increase in the incidence of obesity and its prevalence has been observed in children and adolescents. A child is classified obese when his body weight has more than 25% fat for boys, and 32% fats for girls.

Health risks in obese children

- It is seen that obese children have higher than average blood pressure, and heart rate as compared to children with normal body weight.
- In obese children glucose intolerance and insulin levels are higher than average.
- Weight stress in the joints of the lower limbs are common.
- Poor self-esteem, negative self-image, and depression, have been associated with obesity.
- Smoking as a weight control should be discouraged.

Guidance for the parents
- Children should never be put on a weight-loss diet without medical advice as this can affect their growth.

A well-balanced diet for the child

- 'Complex carbohydrates' should provide half the energy in a child's diet.
- Grill or bake foods instead of frying.
- Avoid fizzy drinks that are high in sugar. Substitute them with fresh juices.
- Healthy protein foods like soya, fish, lentils, and poultry can be taken.
- Frozen yoghurt should be an alternative to ice cream. Bagels are an alternative to doughnuts, like kulcha an alternative to bhatura.

Height

A good height is considered as an essential feature of an attractive and impressive personality. People inherit their height from parents or close relatives. The growth hormone released by the anterior pituitary gland in the brain is accountable for the height of an individual. If it is inactive, your height will be short.

Some popular remedies to help increase height are

- Through stretching exercises like pull ups. A child can increase his height upto 3 inches by doing these exercises.

- Number of asanas (postures in yoga) can help a child increase his height. Tadasana is one such posture. In this asana, you stand straight and take your hands over your head. Then you join both the hands, in a way that your arms touch your ears. Balance your weight on your toes. Maintain the posture for 5-10 seconds and return back to the original position. Do the asana, 5 times initially and then slowly increase the frequency.

Suryanamaskar is another asana which the child can perform.

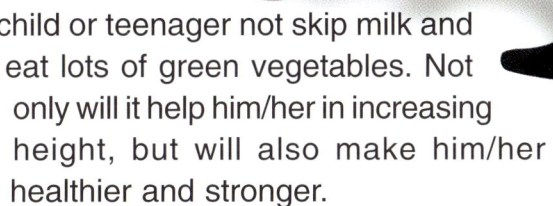

- Having a proper and a well balanced diet goes a long way towards increasing height. A diet rich in proteins, calcium, vitamins, minerals and zinc is essential. Let the child or teenager not skip milk and eat lots of green vegetables. Not only will it help him/her in increasing height, but will also make him/her healthier and stronger.
- Outdoor activities like cycling and swimming on a regular basis help tone up the body.
- Games like tennis or basket ball which require the child to jump and stretch, help in gaining height. Skipping and spot jumping are also good for an increase in height.
- Last but not the least is a proper and sound sleep. It is scientifically proven that when the brain is relaxed, it has a greater capability to release the growth hormone. A tired brain on the other hand, results in an inactive pituitary gland, low release of growth hormone, resulting in shorter height.

Single parenting

Most single parents are females. Single parenting may be associated with numerous problems in children. They can range between social, behavioural and emotional factors. Most children from single parent families do well.

Single parents often discuss almost everything with their children. They share more household responsibilities. This makes the children more independent, mature, resourceful, and responsible.

Myths and Fact File

Despite the vast amount of child health information available to parents today, it remains important to separate fact from fiction. Many myths about caring for children are spread to new parents' by well-meaning family members and friends. Most myths are not harmful but can make it more frustrating to figure out as to how to do the right thing for their child. "Many myths about pediatric care are carried over from generation to generation, and spread by word-of-mouth." "Parents have natural instincts, which combined with medical history of that particular child, are the best advice known to man." says a USA based pediatrician.

Myth

You should not force a picky eater to finish dinner. Forcing a child to eat when he or she isn't hungry may lead to eating disorders later.

Fact

Toddlers often go through periods of refusing to eat certain foods or new foods as a show of independence. Allow experimentation, provide healthy choices, but if your child does not want to eat, don't cook something different for their dinner. Offer a small portion of one or two new foods each week. Limit access to sugary foods and don't provide too much milk or juice so that your child is too full for solids. A small child's diet can be balanced over an entire week rather than every meal, every day.

Myth

Children with a cold should not be given milk or dairy products because it increases mucus production.

Fact

A normal diet can be given to a child when he has developed a cold. Warm foods and drinks would be soothing. If your child does not want to eat, try the BRAT diet which is easy on the digestive system. BRAT stands for bananas, rice, applesauce, and toast.

Myth
Acne is caused by greasy foods and not washing your face.

Fact
Teen acne is caused by inflammation under the skin, generally triggered by fluctuating hormones.

Keeping the skin clean and limiting intake of fatty foods, would always help.

Myth
Watching television stunts a child's brain growth.

Fact
While no research supports this theory, parents should closely monitor the amount and quality of television that their children watch. Too much television contributes to lack of exercise, which can lead to weight problems. Violent action on television and computer games may cause behavior or sleep problems.

Myth
Children need a daily multi-vitamin.

Fact
Most children with a normal diet do not need a multi-vitamin. The average child can get his or her nutritional needs by eating a reasonably balanced diet. Your pediatrician must be consulted before giving your child any type of vitamin or dietary supplement.

Myth
Mother's milk can be avoided. Formula milk today is as good as mother's milk.

Fact
Mother's milk is the best for a baby. It is nutritious, contains globulins which protect a baby from diseases like diarrhoea.

Myth
Polio has been eradicated completely. Children no longer need its vaccine.

Fact
Polio in children has been reduced considerably all over the world, but has not been completely eradicated. In countries like India, it is essential for every child under 5 years of age to receive polio drops according to the regimen set up by the government programme.